Laughter To Get You Through The Day

Jokes & funny sayings to help you keep your sense of humor

Inspired by Faith

Laughter To Get You Throu[gh]
©Product Concept M[fg., Inc.]

D1057219

Laughter To Get You Through The Day
ISBN 978-0-9991681-3-4

Published by Product Concept Mfg., Inc.
2175 N. Academy Circle #200, Colorado Springs, CO 80909

©2017 Product Concept Mfg., Inc. All rights reserved.

Contributions made by Carolyn Hoppe, N.L. Roloff, Patricia Mitchell,
and Vicki Kuyper in association with Product Concept Mfg., Inc.

Scriptures taken from the Holy Bible,
New International Version®, NIV®.
Copyright © 1973, 1978, 1984 by Biblica, Inc.™
Used by permission of Zondervan.
All rights reserved worldwide.
www.zondervan.com

Sayings not having a credit listed are contributed by writers
for Product Concept Mfg., Inc. or in a rare case,
the author is unknown.

Drag your thoughts away from your troubles...
by the ears, by the heels, or any other way you can manage it.

Mark Twain

It's time for a break—a laughter break! Because laughter—a smile, a chuckle, a grin of recognition—has a way of putting problems in perspective, making molehills out of mountains, and giving your heart, mind, and soul a breath of fresh air.

Laughter to Get You Through the Day is a little book guaranteed to bring you great fun. Flip to any page for a joke, one-liner, quip, or cartoon sure to tickle your funny bone—and perhaps someone else's too! These tidbits are made for sharing!

So relax, de-stress, and get your laughter on every day!

Truisms

The old believe everything, the middle-aged suspect everything, and the young know everything.

The shortest distance between two points is usually under construction.

Push will get you almost anyplace you want to go— except through a door marked Pull.

If the grass is greener on the other side of the fence, you know that your neighbor's water bill is higher than yours.

Curiosity is a wonderful quality to have— unless you're a cat.

The chance that you'll have food stuck between your front teeth is directly proportional to the importance of the occasion.

"My wife says I talk in my sleep.
But I'm skeptical.
No one at work has ever mentioned it."

Feeding the Sheep

One Sunday morning, the pastor of a small country church woke to find a night-long blizzard had left snow piled up to his windowsills. As far as he could see, there was nothing but deep snow all around. Although he doubted any of his parishioners would make it to church that morning, he nonetheless dug his way out of his home, braved an icy wind, and trudged through the snow to his church. He sat quietly and waited as service time came and went. Just as he was about to get up to leave, one shivering, snow-covered parishioner appeared at the door.

"Ah, Thomas, you made it!" the pastor said. "But I'm canceling the service, as you're the only one here."

"Pastor," Thomas replied as he sat down. "If a man has a hundred sheep, but only one comes home in the evening, wouldn't he feed it?"

The analogy so inspired the pastor that he ran to the pulpit and launched into his sermon. In his enthusiasm, the minister covered everything he could think of, from Genesis to Revelation. "Amen!" he declared at last. And facing Thomas, he said, "So, what do you think?"

"If a man has a hundred sheep," Thomas replied, "but only one comes home in the evening, does he feed it all the hay in the barn?"

Bats in the Belfry

Three ministers were having lunch when one said, "I'm having a real problem with bats in the church building. They're in the bell tower, in my office, in the fellowship room, and even in the sanctuary! I simply can't get rid of them!"

"Let me tell you about the bats in my church!" the second minister said. "They're hanging from the ceiling, flying through the hallways, and roosting on the rafters. I've tried all kinds of things to scare them away, but nothing works."

"Here's what I did to solve the bat problem in my church," the third minister said. "I simply made them members of the congregation, and I gave each one a box of offering envelopes. Haven't seen one of those critters in my church since."

Keep a Song in Your Heart!

Marriage is like singing in an opera –
it looks easy until you try it!

**The soprano in our neighborhood has extraordinary
range—you can hear her four blocks away!**

Have you heard about the baritone who couldn't find a singing
partner? He ended up buying a duet yourself kit.

**The tenor's recital received mixed reviews—
he liked it, but his audience didn't.**

In Sunday's bulletin: Last week, the choir sang, "I Shall Not Pass
This Way Again," much to the delight of the congregation.

**His voice filled the hall with music! In fact,
most of the audience left to make room for it.**

What's called rock concerts nowadays used
to be called "disturbing the peace."

**A choir member couldn't make it to evening rehearsal—
that morning she had yelled at her kids through the screen
door and strained her voice.**

The way he sings, he could take the role of a pirate in an opera.
He's murder on the high Cs.

She wants to hit the high notes.

Between Friends

"I climb mountains because they're there!"
boasts the hiker.
"Because they're there," replies his less athletically
inclined friend, "is why most people go around them."

Millie announces to her girlfriend, "You know, a lot of
men are going to be miserable when I marry!"
"So," says Tillie, "exactly how many men
do you plan to marry?"

Two middle-aged women are talking.
One says, "I wonder if my husband will love me when
my hair turns gray."
"I don't see why not," says the other. "After all, he's
loved you through six shades already."

"See that woman over there?" a gal says to her friend,
"She's been married four times! First to a millionaire,
second to an actor, third to a minister,
and fourth to an undertaker."
"I know," replies her friend. "One for the money, two for
the show, three to get ready, and four to go!"

Wayne sensed the squirrels were becoming more aggressive.

 **For the Birds**

**Why does a chicken coop have two doors?
Because if it had four it would be a
chicken sedan.**

Chickens are the only animals we eat before they're
born and after they're dead.

**How did the pigeon get to the vet?
Flu.**

Why did the turkey cross the road?
To prove he wasn't chicken.

**Why did the chicken cross the playground?
To get to the other slide!**

Why did Mozart sell all his chickens?
They kept shouting, "Bach! Bach!"

**How do you catch a unique bird?
Unique up on it!**

God Is Everywhere

One evening, Mom asked her young daughter to go to the basement and get a broom. As the shadowy catch-all space was not her favorite place even in the daytime, the girl hesitated. "Don't worry," her mother said, "Jesus is there, even in the darkness." So the girl reluctantly took three steps downstairs and then stopped. "Jesus," she called, "if you're there, would you hand me the broom, please?"

Words to the Wise

If at first you don't succeed...call it Version 1.0.

Teach a man to fish...
and you'll never again get him to buy your fish.

Idle hands are...a sure sign there's no wi-fi.

If you can smile when things go wrong...
you know who's to blame.

Time...wounds all heels.

A picture is worth...a lot of money at auction.

Money can't buy happiness...unless you know where to shop.

Two wrongs...are only the beginning.

The grass is always greener...on the golf course.

Strike while...the fly is on the wall.

No news is...impossible.

If at first you don't succeed...power off, then power on again.

"I joined an on-line dating service and said that I liked swimming and formal wear. They've matched me up with a penguin."

"ROOT VEGETABLES"

Newfangled Invention

An Amish boy and his father were visiting a mall for the first time. They were amazed by everything, but especially by two shiny silver walls that moved apart and then slide back together. "What's that, Father?" the boy asked.

The father, never having seen an elevator before responded, "I've never seen anything like it. I have to admit I don't have any idea what it is." While they were standing there, an elderly woman in a wheelchair rolled up to the moving walls and pushed a button. The walls opened and she rolled into a small room. The walls closed and the father and son watched the numbers above the doors light up sequentially until they reached the highest number. Then, the numbers began to light up in reverse order. When the numbers once again reached 1, the doors opened and a beautiful young woman stepped out.

The father turned to his son and said quietly, "Go get your mother."

Aging Isn't for Sissies

Three unmarried sisters, aged 92, 94 and 96 lived together in the very same house they'd grown up in. One night, the 96-year-old ran a bath. She put her foot in and then paused. "Was I getting in the bath or out of it?" she called down the stairs to her sisters.

The 94-year-old yelled back, "I don't know. I'll come up and see." She starts up the stairs and then pauses. "Was I going up the stairs or down?" she calls out to her sisters.

The 92-year-old who is enjoying a cup of tea at the weathered wooden table in the kitchen shakes her head and says to herself, "I sure hope I never get that forgetful, knock on wood." She then yells to her sisters, "I'll come up and help you both, as soon as I see who's at the door!"

Bumper Stickers

So many clowns, so few circuses.

Gone crazy—back tomorrow.

Reality is a nice place to visit, but I wouldn't want to live there.

**This truck has been in 15 accidents
and hasn't lost one yet.**

I'm not a complete idiot—some parts are missing.

**Ever stop to think and then have trouble
getting started again?**

Student Driver—evacuate the road!

Don't drive like an idiot—I'm much better at it!

I plan to live forever. So far, so good.

No honking—you might wake driver.

Give a man an inch, and he thinks he's a ruler.

A balanced diet is a cupcake in each hand.

"I'd like to open a joint account with someone who has a lot of money."

Guidance from Above

A church member volunteered to do some cleaning around the church one Saturday morning. As he approached the janitor's closet, he found it secured with a padlock. He walked to the office and asked Pastor for the combination. "Well, I'm not sure," the minister said. "Let me have a look at it." As the minister took the padlock in his hand, he lifted his eyes upward and muttered a few numbers, then spun the dial and the lock snapped open.

The volunteer was astonished. "I've never seen such powerful faith!" he exclaimed.

"Not really," the minister replied with a smile. "As soon as I lifted the padlock, I remembered that the combination is written on the ceiling!"

Clothes Closet

A young boy opened the big Bible that had been in the family for several generations. He studied with fascination all the passages his ancestors had underlined, and examined the small, cursive notes crammed in the margins. While he was turning pages, suddenly a dozen dry oak and maple leaves fluttered to the ground.

"Oh, look, Mom!" he called out in delight. "I found where Adam and Eve kept their clothes!"

Something Special for You

A woman walked into a pet shop and said she wanted to buy a sweater for her dog. The assistant showed her a large display of canine garments, and the woman took her time examining several items.

"I just don't know," she said at last, "if I should take a small or a medium."

"You can bring your dog in and we can see which one fits the best," suggested the assistant.

"Oh, dear," said the customer, "I wouldn't want to do that. It's a gift, you see, and I want it to be a surprise."

Good Choice

Once upon a time in a royal palace, the court jester told a joke that the king found insulting. The king ordered him hung without delay. Hearing this, the jester broke down in tears, offered a heart-wrenching apology, and pleaded for mercy. His words softened the king.

"You have served me well for many years," the king said, "and since I am a man of compassion, I give you leave to choose the method by which you shall die."

"Sire," the jester said, "you are indeed most compassionate. I choose to die, therefore, of old age."

"He's fun, funny, handsome,
and a great
conversationalist...
but he's a tennis player,
and love means nothing to him."

Gotcha!

One morning, an elementary school teacher was running late for school. In her anxiety to make it on time, she was driving too fast and raced toward an intersection with a yellow light. Unfortunately, the light turned red just as she entered. A state trooper saw her, flagged her down, and wrote her a ticket.

When her court date arrived, she appeared before the judge and said, "Your Honor, I'm a good driver, and this is the first time I've ever gotten a ticket. I'm a school teacher, and I'm hoping I can attend traffic school instead of paying a heavy fine."

"School teacher, huh?" the judge said as his face broke into a huge grin.

"I've been waiting for an opportunity like this. You are to attend traffic school...and write 'I ran a red light and I will never do it again' 500 times!"

"I have an attitude,
and I know how to use it."

Age Happens

A customer at a garden shop said to the cashier, "I'd like four of those pink flamingos, two giant pinwheels, three spinning sunflowers, one gnome and one of those bent-over grannies in bloomers for my yard."

The cashier responded, "That'll be twenty dollars for the flamingos, ten dollars for the pinwheels, twenty-one dollars for the spinning sunflowers, nineteen ninety-five for the garden gnome and an apology for my wife!"

In Good Time

Two elderly women were playing cards, something they'd done together for years. One day as they were playing, one of them said, "Please don't get mad, but for the life of me I can't remember your name! Please tell me what it is again."

The other woman glared at her friend, silently. Several minutes went by. Finally she said, "Uh, how soon do you need to know?"

How'd You Like to Live Here?
(Real Cities and Towns in the U.S.)

Bummerville, California

Constant Friendship, Maryland

Disco, Illinois

Stop, Kentucky

Frog Jump, Tennessee

Fussville, Wisconsin

Goose Pimple Junction, Virginia

Mosquitoville, Vermont

Nameless, Tennessee

Puddle Town, Connecticut

Roaches, Illinois

Two Egg, Florida

Sweet Lips, Tennessee

Why, Arizona

Zzyzx, California

How Do You Want That?

A traveler sat down in a café for dinner. He ordered the "budget steak," a steak at half the price. Yet when the traveler saw the waiter bring his dinner with his thumb planted squarely in the middle of the steak, he was appalled.

"Why is your finger on my steak?" he demanded.

"Sir," the waiter replied calmly, "you wouldn't want it falling on the floor again, would you?"

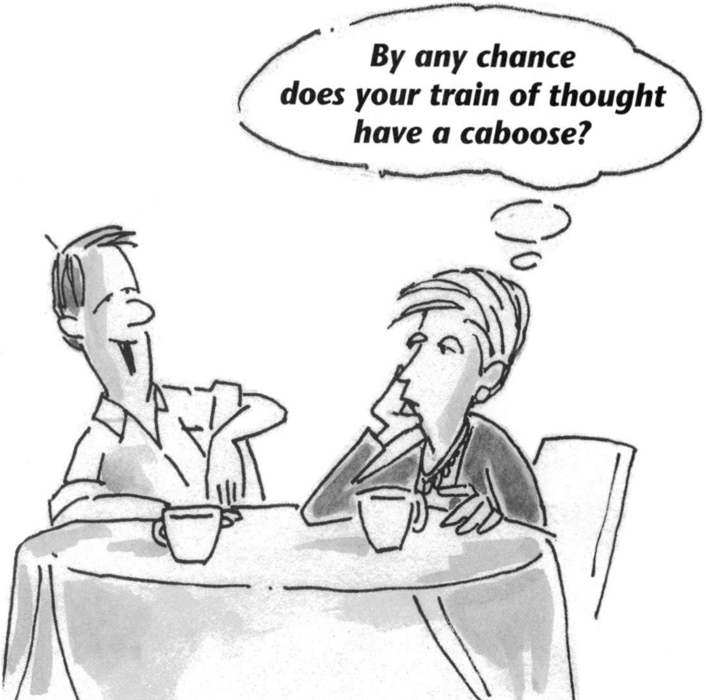
By any chance
does your train of thought
have a caboose?

I used to...

...work in a blanket factory, but it folded.

...sell shoes, but my boss gave me the boot.

...like carpentry, but then I got bored.

...sell computer parts, but eventually I lost my drive.

...enjoy fishing before I was caught playing hooky.

...teach high school, but discovered I didn't have
   enough class.

...run marathons, but couldn't stand the agony
   of de feet.

...work for the railroad until they realized that
   I wasn't trained.

...manage a gym, but found I wasn't fit for the job.

...like being a CPA until it got too taxing for me.

...think I wanted to be a seismologist, but the
   whole profession is on shaky ground.

Signs of the Times

Sign on a Jeweler's Shop:
If your watch doesn't tick, tock to us.

Sign at Whittler's Convention:
We don't care where the chips fall.

Sign outside Oceanography Class:
Open only to students who operate above C-level.

Sign at Maternity Hospital:
Welcome to the Heir Port

Sign on Vegetable Stand:
Take lettuce from the top or heads will roll!

Ditzy Definitions

Reality: that annoying time between waking up and
internet access

**Adult: person who has stopped growing at both
ends and is now growing in the middle**

Ukulele: Missing link between noise and music

**Smile: a curve that can set many
things straight**

Vegetarian: a person who won't eat any
animal that can be seen without a microscope

Avoidable: what a bullfighter tries to do

Cashew: the sound of a nut sneezing

Alarms: an octopus

Baloney: where some skirt hemlines lie

Egotist: someone who's always me-deep in conversation

Heroes: what a guy in a boat does

Giraffiti: spray painting very, very high

Donation: a country of female deer

Aftermath: the class following algebra

Tangent: a fellow who's been in the sun

Deja-stew: leftovers

Meanderthal: a very slow caveman

Lucille: aquarium escapee

**"We both went into
the dryer together,
but I came out alone!"**

Little Misunderstanding

Twelve-year-old Brian wanted to earn some spending money over summer vacation, so he started knocking on his neighbors' doors and asking if they had chores he could do. Mr. Pritchard, who lived three doors down was more than happy to help him out.

"I need someone to paint my porch," he told Brian. "I have the paint in the garage. You'd just need to do the work. How much would you charge for that?" "Thirty dollars," Brian answered.

Knowing that he'd save himself some time and that he'd help keep Brian occupied, Mr. Pritchard hired him on the spot. He brought out the paint and a brush and handed them to Brian.

"I'll be working in the backyard," he said. "Just come on back when you're done." In what seemed like a relatively short time, Brian was at the back gate with an empty paint can.

"Finished!" he said proudly. "I even used the leftover paint to put on a second coat."

"Wow," Mr. Pritchard responded, "that was fast!" "Oh, and by the way," Brian added, "It's not a Porch. It's a Lexus."

"Archie, have you seen your little sister anywhere?"

Why Learning English Isn't Easy...

The farm used to produce good produce.

We must polish the Polish furniture.

The dump was so full it had to refuse more refuse.

The doctor wound the bandage around the wound.

When shot at, the dove dove for the bushes.

Who could object to the beautiful object?

She shed a tear over the tear in her wedding gown.

He could lead well if only he could get the lead out.

"A helpful little tip from me to you: Aways keep several get well cards on the mantle. That way if unexpected guests arrive they'll think you've been ill and unable to clean the house!"

"Don't worry about bird flu," the nurse told me.
"It's completely tweetable."

My friend kept annoying me with bird puns, but then I realized that toucan play at that game.

The chemistry teacher told a joke, but got no reaction.

A courtroom artist was arrested today, but details are still sketchy.

Writing with a broken pencil is simply pointless.

The math instructor turned to the chalkboard and did a number on it.

Fish in schools will sometimes take de-bate.

A book fell on my head, but I've only got myshelf to blame.

Location, Location, Location!

A group of psychology students from around the country were at an educational conference. In an "Emotional Extremes" class, the professor explained, "Before we get into the clinical portion of our lecture, let's establish a baseline for what we'll be discussing." He turned to a student from New York and asked, "What's the opposite of joy?"

"Sadness," she responded.

Next, he asked a student from California, "What's the opposite of depression?"

The young man answered, "Elation."

Then the professor turned to a student from Texas and asked, "And the opposite of woe?"

She replied with a smile, "I believe that would be giddy-up!"

***Sometimes you're the
windshield and sometimes you're...
well, you know.***

"Men have got it made.
They get to DECIDE whether or not
they want to grow a mustache!"

All in the Family

A woman walked into the kitchen and found her husband sneaking around with a fly swatter. "What are you doing?" she asked.

"Hunting flies!" he replied.

"Kill any?" she asked.

"Yup, 3 males, 2 females," he responded.

"How can you tell them apart?" she asked.

He responded, "3 were on the computer and 2 were on the phone."

Ridiculous Laws Still on the Books

In Lynn, Massachusetts,
it's illegal to give a child a cup of coffee.

**If you live in Saco, Missouri,
you're not allowed to wear a hat
that will frighten a child.**

It's illegal to stop a child from jumping
over a puddle in Hanford, California.

**In Washington state it's against the law to pretend
your parents are rich.**

In Gary, Indiana, you cannot attend a theater production
within four hours of eating garlic.

**It's illegal on Sunday afternoon to play hopscotch
on the sidewalk in the state of Missouri.**

A kiss may not last for more than
a second in Halethorpe, Maryland.

It's the Season!

Five-year-old Lyle and his parents were having Thanksgiving dinner at Grandma's house. After the family was seated and the food served on each plate, Lyle started digging in.

"Just a minute!" exclaimed his horrified mother. "Wait until we've said our mealtime prayer, just like we do at home!"

"I didn't think we needed to," Lyle replied.

"Why ever not?" asked his mother.

"Because this is Grandma's house, and she knows how to cook!"

A Sunday school teacher pointed to the American flag on Independence Day and asked, "What flag is this?" One of her little pupils answered, "The flag of our country." "Excellent," said the teacher. "And what is the name of our country?" "Tis of thee," replied the pupil.

An Irishman proposed to his gal on St. Patrick's Day and presented her with a fake diamond. Indignant, she exclaimed, "Are you so cheap that you won't get me even a little real diamond?"

"But it's St. Patrick's Day," he said, "so it's a sham-rock!"

Let the Punishment Fit the Crime

After God created Adam and Eve, He said, "Do not eat the fruit of the tree in the middle of the garden."

Adam demanded, "How come?"

Eve whined, "Why can't we?"

"Because I'm your Father, and I said so!" With that, God left them alone in the garden. Immediately, Adam and Eve eyed the tree and then looked at each other.

"I dare you to take a bite," challenged Eve.

"I dare you," replied Adam.

"No, you first."

"Say, are you chicken or something?" sneered Adam.

"I'm not chicken," yelled Eve as she yanked a fruit off the tree, bit into it, and thrust it at Adam, who took an even bigger bite.

Right then, God returned. Catching both Adam and Eve with a mouthful of forbidden fruit, He was furious. "Didn't I tell you not to eat the fruit of this tree?"

Nearly choking on the fruit as they gulped it down, both nodded "yes."

"Then why did you do it?"

"I dunno," said Adam.

"I dunno," said Eve.

"But she started it!" Adam announced.

"Did not!" Eve shouted.

"Did too!" Adam snapped.

"DID NOT!"

"DID TOO!"

God clapped His hands to His ears. And then He meted out their punishment. He said, "You, Adam and Eve, now shall have children of your own."

Love and Marriage

A husband was telling his buddy about an argument he and his wife had the night before. "It ended, though, when she came crawling to me on her hands and knees," he said.

"Is that so?" replied his buddy with admiration. "What did she say?"

"She said, 'Get out from under that bed, you coward!'"

Ron and Ellen had been dating for over six months when Ellen said to her mother, "Every week, Ron gives me another expensive gift! How can I get him to stop spending so much money on me?"

"Marry him," her mother replied.

After their 60th Anniversary, the husband took to calling his wife by pet names, such as Kitten, Sweetheart, Darling, and Honeybunch. A friend of his was impressed how after all their years of marriage, he spoke so tenderly about his wife.

"To be honest," the husband confessed, "I forgot her name five years ago."

Now I See

A snake slithered to the optometrist's office and said, "My eyesight is getting so bad that I can't see well enough to find my way around anymore. Can you fit me with a pair of glasses?"

"Sure," replied the optometrist, and the snake returned to his home with a pair of glasses that gave him 20/20 vision. It was then he realized that the unfriendly neighbor who wouldn't even say "hi" was a garden hose.

Be Polite

Mom took her young daughter to the doctor's office to get a shot. As soon as the little girl saw the nurse pick up the needle, she broke into a loud wail.

"No! No! No!" she screamed at the top of her lungs.

"Now, now," cajoled her mother, "that's not what we say, is it?"

With barely a pause, the girl shrieked, "No, thank you! No, thank you! No, thank you!"

Where'd You Put Them?

While his son did his geography homework, his dad sat at the computer scrolling through his email. "Hey, Dad," the boy said, "where are the Andes?"

"Go ask your mom, son," he replied distractedly. "She puts everything away in this house."

The Best Gift

One Christmas, three brothers, each one a wealthy and successful executive, wanted to show their mother how much they appreciated her. The eldest had a mansion built for her, and the middle brother bought a luxury car for her. The youngest, knowing that his mother's sight was failing and that she loved to read the Bible, found the perfect gift—a parrot trained to recite any book of the Bible upon request. "It took Bible scholars ten years to train this parrot," he reported to his brothers. "I paid $100,000 for him, but it was worth it."

After Christmas, Mom sent out her thank-you notes. To her eldest son she wrote: "The house is beautiful, but, you know, I have trouble getting around these days, so I use only one room. But I appreciate the thought."

To her middle son she wrote: "The automobile is lovely, but I'm not driving anymore and I have everything I need delivered. Thank you, though."

To her youngest she wrote: "I'm thrilled with the chicken—it was delicious! Thank you so much!"

You're getting up there when...

...it takes ten minutes of scrolling down on a website to find the year you were born.

...you realize it's not your age, but the maintenance, that wears you out.

...you can remember a time when you could go from morning to night without letting all your friends and acquaintances know what you did that day.

...the band you followed from sports arena to sports arena in high school now plays retirement communities.

...you want to live a long life, but you're not keen on this aging thing.

...you start listening when you hear someone talk about knee surgery.

...retirement age isn't the question; retirement income is.

As I Suggested...

The overly confident golfer and his caddy were standing on the tee of a long par three. After surveying the distance, the golfer said, "This looks like a 4-wood and a putt to me."

His caddy politely suggested that he play it safe and hit a 4-iron and then a wedge. His ego bruised, the golfer growled at his caddy, informing him in no uncertain terms that he was equal to any pro and knew precisely what he was doing. So the caddy said no more and handed the golfer the 4-wood he had asked for. The player immediately topped the ball and watched in dismay as it rolled about fifteen yards off the front of the tee.

"It looks like it will be one long putt," the caddy commented as he pulled the putter out of the bag.

A farm hand was seeing his doctor.
"Any accidents since I last saw you?"
the physician asked.

"Nope," the farm hand replied, "nary a one."

"No cuts or bruises?"

The patient thought a minute and then said,
"Well, last summer a rattlesnake bit me on the
ankle. And then during a rodeo,
a bronco kicked me in the ribs."

The physician looked at him in astonishment.
"Wouldn't you call those accidents?"
the physician asked.

"No, doc," the farm hand replied,
"I'm pretty certain those two ornery critters
did it on purpose."

What You Never Want to Hear in the Operating Room!

"I barely made it through med school."

"I left my glasses at home this morning."

"Hmmm...looks like this is going to be a learning experience for all of us."

"Now, what is it—left or right side?"

"How many people have actually survived this, anyway?"

"Might have had a bit too much coffee this morning, because my hand is shaking."

"Hey, let's hurry this up, guys— I don't want to miss my tee time!"

Hey, Baby!

When they brought their first baby home from the hospital, Mom said to Dad, "Honey, why don't you try changing the baby's diaper?"

"I'm busy right now," Dad replied, "but I'll do the next one."

Several hours later, Mom asked again, "Darling, how about changing the baby's diaper?"

"No," replied Dad, "I meant the next baby!"

Wife, three months along, says to her husband, "I wonder when our baby will move?"

"With any luck," Husband replies, "right after he finishes college."

Three men were talking about coincidences, and the first said, "While my wife was pregnant, she read *A Tale of Two Cities*, and then gave birth to twins!"

The second man said, "While my wife was pregnant, she read *The Three Musketeers*, and she gave birth to triplets!"

The third man sprang up in terror. "I've got to get home right now! My wife is pregnant, and she's reading *Ali Baba and the 40 Thieves!*"

Exercise for Couch Potatoes

To help tone those sagging underarms, here's an exercise designed for couch potatoes. Begin by standing on a comfortable surface, with plenty of room on either side to move your arms. With a 5 lb. potato sack in each hand, extend your arms straight out from your sides and hold them there for as long as you can.

Try to reach a full minute, then relax. Each day, you'll find that you can hold this position a bit longer. Repeat this exercise at least three times a week.

After a couple of weeks, move up to 10 lb. potato sacks. Then 50 lb. potato sacks. Eventually try to work your way up to where you can hold a 100 lb. potato sack in each hand with your arms straight out to the side for more than a full minute.

When you reach this stage, move on to the next level. Put a potato in each of the sacks.

On the Job

Interviewer: Why did you leave your last job?
Applicant: Because the company moved
and didn't tell me where.

A manager with a reputation for irritability is asked
by a concerned friend how he deals with job-related
stress. "I don't deal with it at all,"
the manager replies gruffly, "I cause it!"

A man takes great pleasure in telling people that his
job has him deeply involved with Denmark and Brazil.
It's true—every morning, he brings his boss an
apple Danish and a cup of coffee.

The boss strolls through his department one day
and abruptly stops at the desk of an employee
who's watching a series of cute kitten videos on his
computer. "Why aren't you working?" asks the boss.
"Well," replies the employee, "it's because
I didn't see you coming."

To Err Is Human...

If a chef makes a mistake, it's an Exotic Dish

If a chemist makes a mistake, it's a Daring Experiment.

**If an engineer makes a mistake,
it's an Exciting Innovation.**

If a hair stylist makes a mistake,
it's a Trend-Setting Creation.

**If a professor makes a mistake,
it's an Engaging Theory.**

If a driver makes a mistake, it's a New Route.

If your boss makes a mistake, it's a Brilliant Idea.

If you make a mistake, it's a Big Mistake. Period.

Useful Knowledge

A college student worked part-time at a local pizza parlor delivering pizzas. One evening he had to go to the house of a woman notorious among the drivers for her skimpy tips. As he handed her her order, she said grumpily, "I suppose you would like a tip."

"Yes, ma'am, it would be appreciated," said the student, "but the other drivers told me that I'd be lucky to get so much as a quarter from you."

The woman bristled at the accusation. "Just to show you how wrong they were, here's $5!"

"Thank you, ma'am!" said the student. "This will go toward my college expenses."

"What are you studying?" asked the woman.

"Applied psychology," he said with a smile.

Teenagers

Mike: I'm not going out with Karen anymore.
Alan: How come?
Mike: Because she asked me if I knew how to dance.
Alan: So what's wrong with that?
Mike: I was dancing with her at the time.

Son: Dad, it's about my allowance. It's fallen below the national average for teenagers.

Boy: Why won't you go out with me?
Is there someone else? Girl: There's got to be.

Student via text message:
Mom, Dad, I haven't heard from you for a while. Please mail me a check so I know you're okay.

Jill: There's never a dull moment when I go out with Jim.
It lasts the whole evening.

Mom: What's it like to raise a teenager?
Grandma: Multiply the terrible two's by ten and add a driver's license.

*"All I had was a mild headache
until I broke my wrist trying
to open the aspirin bottle!"*

Good Question

It was final exam time, and four off-campus college roommates were serious procrastinators when it came to studying for tests. The day before testing, they finally decided to crack the books, cramming until dawn, and then fell asleep exhausted, until 6:45 a.m. Trouble is, they had forgotten to study one of the subjects, and the exam for it was scheduled for 7 a.m. They quickly put together a plan.

They rubbed motor oil on their hands and wiped their hands on their clothes. Then they waited until the exam was nearly over, drove to campus, and rushed into the classroom. "We're really, really sorry, Professor," they panted, "but we had a flat tire on our way here and had to stop to fix it. Is there any way we can take the exam tomorrow?"

The professor calmly looked at the students, thought a few moments, and said, "Yes, I think that could be arranged. Come to my office tomorrow at this time and I'll let you take your exam."

They were delighted for the extra time, and leaving the classroom, they high-fived one another for having pulled off such a clever ruse. That day, they completed their other exams, went home, and spent the night boning up on the one remaining subject.

Returning to campus the next day, they appeared at the professor's office as instructed. He sat the four students in separate rooms, collected their electronic devices, and gave each one an exam consisting of two questions. The first question, worth 5 points, was easy to answer, and all four breezed through it. The second question, worth 95 points, read: "Which tire was it?"

Things That Make You Wonder Why

You've lugged dozens of boxes of family mementoes and collector's items through countless moves so you could pass them on to your kids. But now they're into the tiny-house movement and living in a space barely bigger than one of the boxes.

You're kneading bread dough and up to your elbows in flour, and that's when your nose starts running.

When you have only one hand free to unlock a door, the keys are always hiding somewhere at the bottom of your purse.

When you eat a piece of chocolate cake, crumbs fall all over the place; but all the calories gather in one place.

After all the new and improved pain relievers, we still have headaches.

The kids have been playing quietly for an hour, but the moment you sit down and get comfortable is when a fight breaks out.

Lesson Learned

One afternoon, a junior staffer, a department manager, and their boss were walking through a park on their way back from lunch. When they spotted something metallic lying under a bush, the junior staffer bent down to pick it up. Turns out it was an antique lamp, and a genie appeared. The genie looked at them and said, "Normally, anyone who finds my lamp gets three wishes; but since there are three of you, I'll grant you one wish each."

The junior staffer excitedly shouted, "Oh genie, my fondest wish is to be on a Caribbean beach with nothing to do but watch the waves." Immediately, the junior staffer vanished.

The department manager couldn't wait to have his wish granted, so he exclaimed, "Oh genie, my fondest wish is to be a rich man on the top floor of a penthouse in a major city." Immediately, the department manager vanished.

The boss turned to the genie and calmly said, "Genie, I wish you'd get those two back here right now." And immediately they were back.

Moral of the story: Let the boss talk first.

(Not) Par for the Course

A golfer decided to take his young son to watch while he played a round of golf, hoping to pique the boy's interest in the game. The round started out badly, however. On the first hole, Dad messed up his tee shot, had to retrieve the ball from a stand of dense bushes, fish it out of a muddy pond, and take several swings to free it from a sand trap. Finally, after half-dozen putts, the ball rolled to the hole and disappeared.

"Oh, no!" cried the boy. "Now you'll never ever find it!"

"I look as beautiful
as I was 20 years ago.
It just takes me longer
to get that way."

Advice for Parents

Cleaning your house before your kids leave home is like shoveling the driveway before it has stopped snowing.

There will come a time when your infant will be able to chew solids—
keys, pens, papers, cell phones...

One child makes you a parent. After the second child, you are a referee.

Your kids are growing up when they start to ask questions that have answers.

A child's fastest growing spurts always happen right after you've bought new school clothes.

A recent study shows that time-out is bad for children. Some readers are doubtful, however, because the entire study is written in crayon.

You know your kids are loud when the bowling alley next door calls and asks you to keep the noise down.

Bored-er Collie.

Worry-for-Hire

A graduate interviewed for an accountant position at a small company. The interviewer, an anxiety-laden man, read through the resume and then turned his attention to the applicant.

"I see you have a degree in accounting, and that's what I'm looking for," he said.

"But just as important is having someone to do my worrying for me."

"Your worrying, sir?" the applicant said.

"Yes, in this business, there are so many things to worry about, and if money isn't one of them, that would be a real relief to me."

"I see," said the applicant. "What does the position pay?"

"I can start you out at a yearly salary of $105,000, plus benefits."

The applicant gasped.

"That's a very generous starting salary, but may I ask, how does such a small company afford that kind of compensation?"

"That," the man said, "would be your first worry."

My Word!

A woman carrying an easel, some paintbrushes, and a palette of paint was going door-to-door through the neighborhood. "Do you know what she's doing?" one neighbor asked another. "Yes," came the reply. "She's canvassing."

A surgeon had worked for years writing a medical textbook, but his editor rejected it. There was a problem with the appendix.

When his son asked if he could have a pet spider, Dad went to the local pet shop and asked how much it would be to buy one. "Fifty dollars," the clerk said. "That's outrageous!" Dad fumed. "I can get one a lot cheaper on the web!"

A man took his car to a garage for routine maintenance. Since earlier he had noticed that one tire appeared low, he asked the mechanic to check it out and add air. When the man went to pay the bill, he was shocked to see a $10 charge for air. "What is this?" he asked. "Air used to be free!" "Well, that's inflation for you," the cashier replied.

Fun Bible Facts

The first bird mentioned in the Bible is a raven.
And he sent forth a raven... (Genesis 8:7)

Manna tasted sweet, like honey wafers.
...and the taste of it was like wafers made with honey.
(Exodus 16:31)

Job's wife thought her husband had halitosis.
My breath is strange to my wife... (Job 19:17)

The shortest chapter in the Bible is Psalm 117,
with only two verses.

The Bible does not say how many Wise Men came to visit
the Baby Jesus. Three is the
traditional number because three gifts—
gold, frankincense, and myrrh—are mentioned.

On One Hand

A boy arrived at school one morning wearing only one mitten. The teacher asked, "Jimmy, why do you have only one mitten?"

"Because I was watching the weather forecast last night," Jimmy replied, "and it said that today would be sunny, but on the other hand, quite cold."

It's a Deal!

On the first day of school, a teacher sent a note home with all her students.

"If you promise not to believe everything your child says happened at school," she wrote, "then I promise not to believe everything your child says happened at home."

How Should I Know?

A man went to the urgent care clinic and told the nurse that he had a bad wasp sting.

"Where is it?" asked the nurse.

Replied the man: "I don't know. It flew away."

Practical Matters First

"Doctor," the patient said, "I'm becoming more and more forgetful. I started out forgetting where I parked the car in parking lots, but now I'm forgetting where I parked it when I've put it in my garage."

"Hmmm," said the doctor. "Before we start treatment, I think you'd better pay me in advance."

Look on the Bright Side

A real estate agent was showing a prospective buyer a new home.

"I like to be honest with people," the agent said, "and I'm going to share with you not just the pluses of this property, but the minuses, too."

Looking around at what seemed to be a well-built and spacious home, the client said, "So tell me what's not to like about this house."

"Well," said the agent, looking downcast, "across the field is a manure plant."

"I see," replied the client. "And what are the pluses?"

The agent brightened and announced, "You'll always know which direction the wind is blowing."

Let Sleeping Cats Lie

Two mischievous monkeys were sitting in a tree when they noticed a large lion ambling along the path beneath them. The king of beasts stepped off the path and stopped at the base of the tree, made himself a cozy cushion of leaves, stretched languidly, lay down, and fell into peaceful slumber. One monkey said to the other, "I dare you to go down and tickle that lion on the belly."

"I'll do it," the other monkey said. "I'm not afraid of that old fellow."

With that, the monkey stealthily scampered down the tree, tickled the lion's belly, and then ran off into the jungle. The lion woke up and angrily realized what had happened, so he decided it was time to teach the culprit a lesson. Springing into action, he dashed after the monkey. When the monkey heard the big cat gaining on him, he figured that he'd better act quickly or he would be caught in no time. Spying a newspaper that had been left lying on the ground, he picked it up, leaned against a rock, and started reading.

In a few moments, the lion showed up. "Say," he panted, "did you see a monkey run past you just now?"

The monkey lowered the paper and said, "You mean the monkey that tickled a sleeping lion on the belly?"

"I can't believe it!" cried the lion. "It's hit the media already!"

"Joe says we need to get back to nature, so he wants us to go camping a month this summer. But I told him, 'Joe, I love Mother Nature, too, but I don't see why we have to move in with her.'"

Amenity-Free Establishment

A traveler was checking into a budget hotel when the clerk asked him if he had a good memory for faces.

"Why do you ask?" the man said.

"Because there are no mirrors in the bathroom."

Rooms for Cheap

A traveler was checking into a budget hotel when the clerk said, "Rooms are $50 a night, $25 if you make your own bed."

"Not a problem," replied the traveler, "I'll make my own bed."

The clerk made a note of the guest's choice, and then handed him a hammer, nails, and lumber.

"For our anniversary, we went to that expensive nouveau cuisine restaurant downtown. After spending $200 on dinner, we got home, looked in the refrigerator, and realized that the babysitter had more to eat than we did."

Play Ball!

The kindergarten softball team's game was rained out, so the coach explained that they would schedule a makeup game. One of the boys raised his hand and stated firmly that there was no way he was going to play a makeup game, and that he absolutely would not wear makeup!

Two elderly fans were watching as the football game entered its fourth quarter. One turned to the other and remarked: "I guess we're in our fourth quarter of life."

"Not to worry," his pal said, "maybe we'll go into overtime."

The high school home team was losing big time, and the team's cheerleaders were standing on the sidelines and watching glumly. The coach ran over to them and shouted, "Don't you think you should be out there cheering for your team?"

"I think," one declared, "we should be out there playing for our team!"

You Herd Right

Out in the field, two farmers were talking and the first farmer said:

"I've got a great flock of cows."

" 'Herd' of cows," said the second farmer corrected.

"Of course I've heard of cows," snapped the first. "I've got a whole flock of them!"

Get the Point?

A man came to work wearing a loud shirt and tie in a novelty print.

"What do you think of my new shirt?" the man asked one of his colleagues. "I bought it on our desert vacation, and it has different kinds of cactuses all over it."

"Cacti," corrected his colleague.

"Forget the tie," the man said, "look at the shirt!"

Thanks for the Information

A man had been stranded on a desert island for five years. Finally, he discovered a bottle with a note in it had been washed ashore. With trembling hands, he uncorked the bottle, unfolded the note, and read:

"Due to inactivity, we regret to inform you that your email account has been canceled."

Keeping Up with the Joneses

Bill took pride in his perfectly mown lawn and trimmed bushes. His neighbor, however, was a casual gardener, at best. One day Bill commented to the homeowner that an unkempt yard reflected poorly on the neighborhood.

"Look," the homeowner said, "my yard looks as good as anyone else's after the first good snowfall."

*"I decided I'd trace my family tree.
I never was very good at drawing."*

One Way

A man was strolling along the sidewalk when from around the corner came a crowd of people running toward him.

"Hey, what's going on?" cried the baffled pedestrian to anyone who would listen. Finally one of the runners slowed down long enough to shout, "A lion has escaped from the circus across town!"

"Which direction is he heading?" asked the pedestrian.

"You don't think we're chasing him, do you?"

As Excuses Go...

A long-distance trucker was driving a semi along the highway when he saw a sign that read, "Low Bridge Ahead."

Almost immediately, the bridge appeared right in front of him and he was traveling too fast to stop in time. He hit the bridge and got stuck, backing up traffic for miles. When a state trooper arrived on the scene, he climbed out of his car, looked over the scene, and, with a jaunty air, approached the trucker.

"So," the trooper said, "looks like you got yourself stuck under the bridge."

"Not at all, sir," the trucker replied.

"I was delivering the bridge to a customer, and ran out of gas."

Did you hear the one about...

...the couple who met in a revolving door?
They're still going around together.

...the librarian who's expecting a baby?
Her colleagues are worried about her, though,
because she's two weeks overdue.

...the dieter who discovered that a
camera made her look heavier?
That's when she stopped eating cameras.

...the investor who put all his money
in a candy factory?
He made a mint.

...the lighthouse keeper who raised chickens?
He liked to have eggs with his beacon.

...the dog that gave birth to puppies in the city park?
She was ticketed for littering.

Limited Resources

One day when Noah and his family were in the ark, Noah announced that he was bored and wanted to spend the day fishing. "That's a good idea," said his wife. "Go ahead, and I'll see you at dinner."

So Noah picked up his rod and reel, stepped out of the ark, and began to fish. Thirty minutes later, he was back.

"How come so soon?" asked his wife. "Aren't the fish biting today?"

"They're biting all right," Noah answered, "but I only had two worms."

Fish Tale

A father and son were out in a boat fishing.
"What's the biggest fish you ever caught, Dad."
"Son, I caught one once that was 14 inches."
His son thought about this a minute, and then ventured to say, "That doesn't sound like such a big fish to me."
"That's 14 inches between its eyes, Son."

Very Punny

A church janitor who is also the Sunday organist
always watches his keys and pews.

**Two geologists are examining a wide crevice left by a
recent earthquake. One turns to the other and says,
"It's not my fault."**

A sportscaster's wife just delivered twins.
The new dad was delighted with the infant replay.

**A newspaper reporter insists on wearing no-iron shirts,
citing freedom of the press.**

A shopper considers buying an origami belt, but then
decides against it because it would be a waist of paper.

**A CEO finally realizes that no matter how much she
pushed the envelope, it's still stationery.**

The Visitor

A man flew to a faraway country on business and was greeted at the airport by his friendly and affable host. Together they took a cab to the visitor's hotel, and at the end of the trip, the cab driver asked for ten dollars. Just as the visitor was about to hand over the cash, his host snatched it and angrily yelled at the driver in their native language. At the end of his tirade, the host handed the driver five dollars and scornfully waved him off.

As the cab disappeared around the block, the host turned to the visitor and handed him the rest of the money.

"Those cab drivers will rob you every chance they get. I apologize, sir."

"I understand," said the visitor, "but I think you should know that my luggage is still in the trunk of his cab."

Please Come Over

A stay-at-home mom was having a really rough day. The baby was restless and cranky, and her toddlers wouldn't settle down. She was behind in her housework, hadn't yet done the shopping, and was expecting company at dinner that evening. In the middle of all this, the phone rang. "Hi, daughter," a kindly female voice said.

"I just thought I'd check in and see how you're doing today."

"It's hectic, Mom!" And the harried homemaker proceeded to relate everything that was going wrong and all the work that had yet to be done.

"Let me help, sweetheart," the caller said.

"Give me half an hour, and I'll be over there to watch the kids and tidy up the house while you go to the grocery store."

"You're a lifesaver!"

"And I'll call John and remind him to come home early if your guests are expected at 6."

There was a pause. "John?" the homemaker said. "My husband's name is Bill."

Another pause. "Is this Tracey?"

"No, this is Shelley."

"I'm so sorry," the caller gushed, "but I dialed the wrong number! Please accept my apologies."

"Oh," Shelley said in a thin voice, "so that means you won't be coming over, I guess."

Life in the City

A woman goes into a bank in New York City and asks for a personal loan of $2,000. She tells the loan officer that she's going on a cruise for two weeks and would like to have the money in case an emergency should arise. As collateral, she offers the bank the car she owns, new-model sports car, fully paid for. She produces the title and keys to the car, and the loan officer extends the money. An employee drives the woman's car into the bank's underground garage, and the woman leaves on her cruise.

While she's gone, the employees at the bank take turns admiring the sleek and shiny car, chuckling among themselves at the silliness of using a $30,000 vehicle as collateral for a mere $2,000 loan.

Two weeks later the woman returns to the bank and repays the loan plus $12.50 interest. The loan officer thanks her for her business, but he can't keep himself from saying, "We see on your application that you earn a sizable salary and possess substantial financial assets. Why would someone in your position want to borrow $2,000?"

"I'll tell you," the woman replies, "there's no place else in the City I could park my car for two weeks for $12.50 and know it's safe and secure the whole time."

Occupational Wisdom

Acupuncturists take pride in a jab well done.

Parents are the ones who spend the first two years of
their kids' lives teaching them to walk and talk, and then
the next ten years telling them to sit down and be quiet.

Horticulturists are sure to grow on you.

Optometrists take a vacation whenever
the daily grind gets them down.

**The theater major had a reputation as a drama queen,
and she took it as a compliment.**

Mathematicians know what really counts.

Dentists are used to the drill.

On the Money

A tour guide was leading a group around Washington, D.C., when he pointed to a spot by the Potomac River.

"That's where tradition has it that George Washington was standing when he threw a coin to the other side."

"I don't believe it," scoffed one of the tourists.

"No one could throw a coin that far."

"You have to keep in mind," the guide said, "that money went a lot further back in those days."

Savings Plan

Because his young son was struggling in math class, his father thought he would offer the boy some incentive to do well on the final exam.

"If you get a good grade on the test," his father said, "I'll give you $50."

When test day came, the boy returned from school with a smile on his face.

"Hey Dad," he said, "you'll be glad to hear that I just saved you $50!"

Never Say No

The hardware store manager hired a new sales assistant. After he had been on the job for only three days, the manager overhead him tell a customer, "It's true, we haven't had any for a long time, and I don't think we'll get any in the near future, either."

After the customer left, the manager pulled the new-hire aside.

"Never tell a customer we can't get something," the manager instructed.

"You take down what they're asking for, and I can order it and have it here in a couple days—week at most."

The new-hire nodded and said he understood. Then the manager asked what it was the customer had wanted.

"Rain," replied the new-hire.

"That's all very interesting,
but I was asking about the
birds and the bees because
I have to do a zoology project
for school this semester."

The Jacket

Tom and his wife were cleaning out the basement one day when they came across a box of family mementoes. Rummaging through the contents, Tom happened on a dry-cleaning receipt from ten years ago.

"Now I know what happened to my favorite sports jacket," said Tom with a laugh, "I forgot to pick it up from the dry cleaners! I wonder if it's still there."

"I doubt it," his wife replied.

"Well, let's see, just for fun." With that, Tom put the ticket in his pocket. That afternoon, he went to the dry cleaning establishment and with a straight face, handed the clerk the ticket.

The clerk looked at the ticket and said he'd have to go in the back of the shop. After a few minutes, he shouted,

"Yep, here it is!"

"Seriously?" Tom called to the clerk.

"Who would have thought you'd have kept that jacket after all this time!"

The clerk came back to the counter.

"It'll be ready next Friday," he announced.

Name Game

A boy came home from his first day at school and said to his mother, "Mom, I'm so glad you named me Danny."

"Why is that, honey?"

"Because that's what the teacher and all the kids in my class call me."

It's True

A boy was sitting on the front lawn of a house. A neighborhood canvasser looked at him and asked, "Is your mother home?"

"Yep," said the boy.

The canvasser proceeded confidently up to the front door and rang the doorbell. No answer. After a minute, she rang the doorbell again, but still no answer. As she turned around and walked back to the sidewalk, she said to the boy, "I thought you told me that your mother was at home."

"She is," replied the boy, "but this isn't where I live."

Paving the Way

A woman wanted an attractive path through her rose garden, so she arranged for several hundred decorative pavers to be delivered to her home. She had never put in a path before and intended to find out how to do it, yet when the pavers arrived, she was so excited that she started laying them out right away. By early evening, the path was finished, but she realized that she hadn't prepared the ground and the pavers were uneven. So she took them up and put them in a pile next to her house until the next day.

The next day she raked the ground and laid out the pavers again. When she finished that evening, however, she decided that she didn't like the design, and she wanted to try another design tomorrow. Again she took up all the pavers and put them in a pile next to her house. The next morning, as she was relaying the pavers, a neighbor ambled over and said, "I see you're making a path through your garden."

"That's right," the woman said proudly.

"I was just wondering," said the neighbor, "are you planning on putting it away every night?"

"No one told on you.
I saw the whole thing
on your social media page."

Second Time Around

Two country bumpkins went to the movies to see a Western. Toward the end of the movie, they watched as a cowboy astride a galloping horse headed straight for the edge of a cliff.

"I bet you twenty dollars he goes right over that cliff," said one.

"You're on," said the other.

Within ten seconds, the cowboy disappeared down the cliff. As the second man handed over the money, the first said, "You know, pal, I feel guilty taking your money because I've seen this movie before."

"So have I," the second man said, "but I sure didn't think he'd be dumb enough to go over the cliff a second time."

Heavenly Humor

The church youth group organized a car wash to raise money for their camping trip. They hung a large sign that read, "Car Wash for Youth Camping Trip." In the morning, business was booming and cars were lined up around the block. Around noon, however, the sky darkened and it began to rain. Cars started to pull away, much to the dismay of the washers. All that changed, though, when one of the young people had an idea. She took a marker, reached up to the sign, and added: "We wash, God rinses."

Billy, having misbehaved, was sent to his room for some time-out. When he reemerged, he told his mother that he had thought it over and then said a prayer. "That's very good," said his mother. "If you asked God to help you behave, He will do it."

"That's not what I asked Him," Billy replied. "I asked God to help you put up with me."

The Sunday school teacher was telling the children about Lot's wife, who, upon looking back at Sodom, turned into a pillar of salt. Johnny raised his hand and said, "I know how that is. Yesterday my mom looked back while she was driving, and she turned into a telephone pole."

Little Emma's newborn baby brother was crying up a storm when Emma asked, "Mommy, where did he come from?"

"He came from heaven," her mother replied.

"Oh," said Emma with an understanding nod. "Now I know why they threw him out!"

Cannot Tell a Lie

A little boy was growing up on his parents' farm located far outside of town. He loved everything about rural life, except for having to use an outhouse. It was cold in the winter, hot in the summer, and scary at night.

The outhouse stood on the bank of a stream. One afternoon, the boy decided to get rid of the offending structure by pushing it into the water. Since there had been heavy rain the day before, the stream was swollen, and the boy figured the outhouse would not have far to go if he gave it a few shoves in the right direction. So he shoved, and the outhouse tipped, rolled into the stream, and drifted away in the current.

That evening, his dad came into the boy's room and sat down. "Son," he said sternly, "It seems that someone pushed the outhouse into the stream this afternoon. Was it by any chance you?" Meekly, the boy nodded assent. He thought a moment, and then added, "You know, Dad, when George Washington chopped down the cherry tree, he wasn't punished because he admitted what he did."

"Yes, son," Dad replied, "but George Washington's father wasn't in the cherry tree."

Punny Stuff

An unlucky man sent ten different puns to a contest,
hoping at least one would win.
Sadly, no pun in ten did.

**What do you call someone who
used to be called Lee?
Formerly.**

What happens when seafood tries to dance?
It pulls a mussel.

**Two silk worms had a race,
but both ended up in a tie.**

How to Get Rich

"My philosophy," the successful business executive told a young graduate, "is always to do your best and give your best to your work, because it will bring you more satisfaction than getting a high salary."

Impressed, the graduate said, "Is that what brought you so much wealth?"

"No," replied the executive, "I became wealthy when I was able to convince my employees of that philosophy."

They're After Me

An employee went into the supervisor's office and said, "Boss, I need a raise in salary. And just so you know, there are four companies after me."

"Really?" said the supervisor.

"And may I ask which companies?"

"Gas, water, cable, and electric," the employee said.

"I have the smartest cat in the world. He eats the cheese, then waits at the mouse hole with baited breath."

Uh-Oh

A boy knocked on his neighbor's door. When the homeowner answered the door, the boy said, "There's something of mine in your garage, and I've come to get it back."

Puzzled, the homeowner obliged, opened the garage door, and saw a baseball and a window with a baseball-sized hole in it. Looking at the boy, he said, "Now, how do you suppose your baseball landed in my garage?"

The boy looked at the ball and then at the window. "Wow, a perfect shot! I must have thrown it right through that hole!"

Mom...

A boy approached his mom looking quite sheepish.
"You know that vase you told me has been in the family for many past generations?" he said.

"Yes," his mom replied.

"The present generation just knocked it over."

**"When my toddlers act up,
I use a safe, comfortable playpen.
And when they calm down,
I get out."**

What's That Again?

Bob Miller and Peggy Nichols were married yesterday,
their 10-year friendship ending at the altar.

**The Health and Fitness Club is hosting an all-you-can-eat
pancake breakfast fundraiser this Saturday morning.**

Job posting: Lifeguards. Ability to swim a plus.

**The new medical facility will offer both impatient
and outpatient care.**

For sale: Sofa, chair, and ottoman.
Good condition. Manure color. Will deliver.

**Dr. Ross' seminar attendees learned that "Do Not
Resuscitate" orders put patients at greater risk of death.**

Free to Good Home: Two kittens, one black and white,
the other white and black.

Help Wanted: Experienced prooofreader.

Get the Message?

Coming out of church one summer morning, a woman greeted the minister and said, "That was a marvelous message, Pastor. I found it so helpful."

"I hope you didn't find it as helpful as you found my Christmas message," the minister replied.

"Whatever do you mean by that?" the woman said.

"Because that one seemed to have lasted you for six months."

Morning Prayer

Dear God, I'm doing okay. I haven't gossiped about anyone, nor have I lost my temper with the kids. I haven't coveted something I can't afford, envied a friend's good fortune, and I haven't taken offense at anyone's rudeness or careless remark. I haven't been selfish or discontent, lazy or argumentative. So far, so good!

But now I'm getting out of bed, so please help me, Lord. It's going to be tougher from here on. Amen.

Laughter's in the Air

After every flight, pilots need to inform mechanics if they've noticed any problems with the aircraft. When the mechanics fix the problem, they document their work on a form which the pilots review before taking off on the next flight. Here are a few actual maintenance requests by a pilot (P) and the response by a mechanic (M).

P: Left inside main tire almost needs replacement.
M: Almost replaced left inside main tire.

P: Something loose in cockpit.
M: Something tightened in cockpit.

P: Dead bugs on windshield.
M: Live bugs on backorder.

P: Evidence of leak on right main landing gear.
M: Evidence removed.

P: Suspected crack in windshield.
M: Suspect you're right.

P: Mouse in cockpit.
M: Cat installed.

P: Noise coming from under instrument panel.
   Sounds like a midget pounding on something
   with a hammer.
M: Took hammer away from midget.

P: Aircraft handles funny.
M: Aircraft warned to: straighten up,
   fly right and be serious.

P: Target radar hums.
M: Reprogrammed target radar with lyrics.

The Auction

At an auction, a man saw a beautiful parrot that he decided he wanted. He bid $25, but someone bid $30. He bid $35, but someone yelled out, "Fifty!" This went on for several minutes as the bids escalated, until the man shouted, "Two hundred dollars!" No other bids were heard, and the auctioneer said, "Sold for $200."

When the successful bidder came to pick up the parrot, he said to the auctioneer, "For such an expensive bird, I sure hope he can talk."

"He sure can," came the reply. "Who do you think was bidding against you?"

Here to Buy

A man walked into a hardware store and asked the sales assistant for a bag of nails. "How long do you want them?" the clerk asked.

"Oh," said the man, "I would like to keep them."

Did you hear the one about...

...the romance in the tropical fish aquarium?
It was a case of guppy love.

**...the writer who announced he had written a
best-seller? The only thing he had yet to do is find
some best-buyers.**

...the rocky marriage of the dentist and the
manicurist?
They fought tooth and nail.

**...the woman who was asked by a
passport agent to identify herself?
She dug into her purse, pulled out a mirror,
looked at it, and said, "That's me, all right."**

...the staff member who asked her boss for
more personal recognition?
Her supervisor suggested wearing
a name tag.

**...the woman who went to an unfinished furniture
store? They sold her a tree.**

You know things aren't going well
for yourself when you walk out of a
memory-improvement class
and can't remember where you
parked your car.

Life with Kids

A little boy was raised in an ideal family. He was happy, healthy, and perfectly normal in all ways except one—at five years old, he still hadn't said a word. Then one day at the dinner table, all that changed. "Ugh, this milk doesn't taste very good," he said clearly.

His mother and father were overjoyed to finally hear him speak. "Why did you wait so long to talk to us?" they asked him.

"Up to now," he replied, "everything's been great."

Little Rodney ran out of the bathroom in tears. "What's the matter?" Dad asked.

"I dropped my toothbrush in the toilet!"

"Don't worry, son," Dad said. "I'll just fish it out and we'll throw it away."

When he returned, Rodney was holding up another toothbrush.

"Isn't that mine?" his dad asked.

"Yes," Rodney replied, "and you'd better throw it away, too, because it fell in the toilet last week."

One evening when Mom was out, Dad put Junior to bed and then settled down in front of the TV. But every few minutes, Junior ran out of his room and asked Dad for a glass of water. After the seventh time, Dad lost his temper and yelled, "Go to sleep now! That's the last glass of water."

"But Dad," the boy protested, "my room's still on fire!"

Proverbial Wisdom

The pen is mightier than the sword—
and much easier to write with, too.

**Life is what you make it—which could explain a lot of the
biographies on Internet dating sites.**

If you take the road less traveled, don't be surprised
if you soon will need new shock absorbers.

**Sometimes it's best to swallow your pride—
and don't worry, it's calorie-free.**

Sticks and stones may break your bones,
but words can never hurt you—
unless someone bops you on the head with a dictionary.

**You can't have everything—because if you did,
you'd have no place to put it.**

Practice makes perfect—
but then no one's perfect, so why practice?

*"I've never been overdrawn
at the bank!
Just under-deposited
from time to time."*

Diagnosis

A little girl came home from school one afternoon and told her mother that she had a stomach ache.

"It's just because your stomach is empty, honey," Mom said.

"Sit down and I'll fix you a nice snack, and you'll feel much better." Sure enough, after the girl had eaten her snack, her stomach ache disappeared.

That evening at dinner, Dad mentioned that he'd had a headache all day. The girl perked up.

"Dad," she said, "your head will feel much better after you put something in it."

Sound the Alarm

On the first day of nursery school, the teacher was telling her charges what to do in case of an emergency. She held up a smoke alarm and asked if anyone knew what it was.

"A smoke alarm!" the kids chorused.

"Now can someone tell me what it means when you hear this sound," the teacher said as she pressed the alarm test button.

"It means Daddy's cooking dinner tonight," a little voice piped up.

**The other cat says,
"Doctor, what are you
working on today?"
The first cat answers,
"My usual...String Theory."**

Confident Artist

Mom saw her little daughter with paper and pencil in hand and sitting at the kitchen table. Walking over to the table, Mom asked the girl what she was planning to draw.

"I want to make a portrait of God," the girl answered.

"Why, honey," Mom said with a smile, "God is invisible to human eyes. People don't know what He looks like."

Without looking up from her project, the girl replied: "They'll know when I'm finished."

Reason Why

A teacher asked her preschoolers, "Can a bear take off his warm winter overcoat?"

"No," the kids chorused.

"Why not?" asked the teacher.

Suddenly the room got quiet. Finally, one little voice piped up: "I think it's because only God knows where the buttons are."

All Right with You?

An OB-GYN had worked her way through med school by working part-time in a deli. The new mother couldn't help but notice when the physician delivered her first baby and announced, "It's a little over seven pounds. Is that okay?"

Not Yet?

One evening, a boy went to the hospital to visit his mother and his new twin sisters. On his way out, he stopped in an adjoining room where he saw a woman with her leg in traction.

"How long have you been in the hospital?" the boy asked the woman.

"It's been three weeks," said the woman.

"Then where's your baby?" the boy asked.

"Oh, I don't have a baby."

"You're sure taking a long time," the boy told her.

"My mom came in this morning and she already has two!"

The Invitation

A dentist was working late in his clinic one night when someone knocked at the door. When he opened it, a man said, "Can you help me, doc? I think I'm a moth."

"I'm a dentist," the doctor replied, "and you need to see a psychiatrist."

"Yes, I know that."

"Well, then why did you come here?"

"I was attracted by the light."

You can always pick out...

...the experienced mothers at children's birthday parties. They don't give each child a napkin—they sit all of them on drop cloths.

Remedy

A patient returned to the doctor's office for a follow-up visit. The doctor was puzzled when she saw that her patient's skin rash showed no signs of improvement. "Now you've been applying the ointment I prescribed every day for the past seven days, just like I said, haven't you?"

"No, doctor," the patient replied, "I couldn't. The instructions say 'apply locally,' and I've been out of town all week."

Help!

One morning, a man came into the emergency room.

"What happened?" asked the nurse on duty.

"I was in such a hurry to get to work," the man explained, "that I ran through my screen door and strained myself."

Truisms

You start cutting your wisdom teeth the first time
you bite off more than you can chew.

**Money isn't everything, but it is guaranteed to
keep the kids in touch with you.**

Laugh and the world laughs with you—
cry and you have to blow your nose.

**The person who says that nothing is impossible
has never tried to eat an ice cream cone from
the bottom up.**

The grass is greener on the other side—
but have you ever flipped it over to check?

One good turn gets most of the blankets.

If you can laugh when things go wrong,
you probably don't realize what went wrong.

**When the cat's away, no hair accumulates on
the furniture.**

*"I love to lie on the beach.
Everyplace else,
I tell the truth."*

Daffy-nitions

Electricity: Well-organized lightning.

Budget: A plan to live below your yearnings.

Hard-boiled egg: An egg that's hard to beat.

Carbage: Trash found in an automobile.

Experience: The positive spin we put on our mistakes.

Antique: A piece of furniture that has made a round trip to the attic and back.

Computer: A device that enables you to make errors faster than you could on your own.

Right Way

A boy is standing on the sidewalk outside a dress store while his mother shops. Soon the pastor, new in town, comes by and asks him where Main Street is. The boy points him in the right direction.

"Thanks, son, I appreciate your help," says the pastor.

"Now if you come to my church on Sunday, I'll show you the way to heaven."

"No thanks," says the boy. "You can't even find Main Street!"

Have a Question?

Q: Why are older homeowners so reluctant
to get rid of all the stuff they've stored in their
attics and basements over the years?
A: Because they know that as soon as they do,
their adult kids will want to store stuff there!

Q: How do you get down from an elephant?
A: You don't. You get down from a duck.

Q: What did the French chef give his wife on her birthday?
A: A hug and a quiche!

Q: What did one raindrop say to the other?
A: Two's company; three's a cloud.

Q: Why didn't the skeleton accept the party invitation?
A: He had no body to go with.

# Just Checking

A captain of an ocean liner observed the same ritual for 30 years: Every morning before appearing on deck, he would open his desk drawer, look at a piece of paper, nod, and then close the drawer. Upon the captain's retirement, his assistant, who was aware of the odd habit, finally got a chance to sit at the desk and open the drawer. On it he read: "Port left, starboard right."

Long Commute

An office worker's commute meant that he was on the road two hours in the morning and another two hours in the afternoon. When he complained to a coworker, the coworker suggested that, instead of the car, he take the train.

"That's not for me," the commuter said. "I tried it once, and for the life of me, I couldn't drive the thing."

Long Vacation

"Vacations can last for months," the frequent traveler said to his friend. "You travel in August, return in September, get bills in October, get rested up by November, and find your luggage delivered to your door in December."

Fire!

"My house is on fire!" a woman reported to the fire department. "Please come quickly!"

"We'll be right over," the dispatcher said, "just tell us how to get there."

There was a pause on the line.

"Don't you have those big red trucks anymore?"

Be Quiet!

A small zoo couldn't afford to house a real gorilla, so they hired a man to dress in a gorilla costume and act like a great ape. So the man did, throwing himself into his role with abandon. Visitors laughed and clapped as he ate dozens of bananas, pranced around his enclosure, and thumped his chest dramatically. Then one day, trying a new antic, he accidentally flipped himself into the lion's enclosure.

"Help! Help!" he yelled in terror.

The king of beasts roared, lunged at him, put a paw on his chest and hissed, "Be quiet, or we'll both lose our jobs!"

Mr. Fix-It

Four engineers were carpooling on their way to an industrial complex when their car stalled. The mechanical engineer immediately diagnosed the problem.

"It's the pistons, guys," he said. "Soon as we fix them, we'll be on our way."

"I think it's the spark plugs," countered the electrical engineer. "All we have to do is replace them, and we're good to go."

"Bad gas," volunteered the chemical engineer. "Let's flush the system, fill 'er up, and we're rolling."

The three of them turned to the IT engineer, who so far had not said a word. He shrugged. "Let's get out of the car, slam the doors shut, open them, get in, and try revving it up again."

Problem Solved

"If our computers get too powerful," the programmer announced to his staff, "we'll organize them into committees. That will take care of it."

The Poet

A college freshman and a classmate, madly in love, were strolling along the beach. The young man gazed out at the water and declared with a wide flourish of his hand, "Oh, sea, thou great and mighty force, roll on! Roll on!"

His girlfriend's eyes looked at him admiringly. "Oh, Tom," she said, "you're so wonderful! It's doing it!"

Crazy for You

A sleek tomcat fell in love with the lovely calico next door.

"You're so beautiful," he purred in her ear. "I'd die for you." Coyly she looked at him and said, "How many times?"

My Love

A girl asked her sweetheart, "Do you love me?" "Of course I do, dear," he answered.

"Then would you die for me?" she probed. "Uh—no. My love for you is an undying kind of love."

"I took 'Introduction to Shakespeare' last semester, but it was really disappointing. He never once showed up in class."

How Come?

One day a baby camel came to his mom and said, "Mom, how come I have such large toes?"

"That's so, when you can walk across the desert, your feet won't sink in the deep sand," she answered.

The baby camel thought about this for a minute, decided it made sense, and then asked, "Mom, how come I have such long eyelashes?"

She said, "That's so, when you can walk across the desert, your eyes are shielded from the glaring sun and blowing sand."

The baby camel decided this made sense, too, and he asked yet another question, saying: "Mom, how come I have this big hump on my back?"

Mom smile and said, "That's so, when you walk across the desert, you can go for great distances without water. Isn't it wonderful how we're so well-equipped to travel comfortably across such a harsh landscape as a desert?"

"Yes," replied the baby camel, "but then, Mom, how come we live in a zoo?"

Difficult Jobs

One Sunday, the pastor's sermon lasted an unusually long time and little Kenny got antsy. When at last the service ended and he was in the car with his mom and dad, he said, "Is that all Pastor does is talk on Sunday morning?"

"Oh, no," replied his mother.

"During the week, Pastor visits shut-ins and people in the hospital, helps out at the food pantry, meets with families who need help, and makes sure that the church building is taken care of and everyone is happy."

"That's right," said his father.

"He also needs time to rest up, because speaking in public is not an easy thing to do."

Kenny sighed; "Listening isn't very easy, either."

"I told my kids that when it comes to Christmas presents, money is no object—unless what they want costs too much."

Did you hear the one about...

...the dog that flunked out of obedience school?
He blamed the kids for eating his homework.

**...the chemist who discovered a liquid
that would dissolve anything?
Trouble is, he couldn't find a container to keep it in.**

...the caterpillar that watched a butterfly flutter
and float on the currents of the wind?
He promised himself he'd never,
ever get into one of those contraptions.

**...the fellow who heard that exercise
would add years to his life? After only 20 minutes
at the gym, he felt 15 years older.**

...the two dish antennae that met and got married?
The ceremony was boring,
but the reception was excellent.